POETRY FROM

A FRAGILE

MIND

By

James M. Love

Copyright © James M. Love 2019
This book is sold subject to the condition that it shall not, by way of trade or otherwise, be lent, resold, hired out, or otherwise circulated without the publisher's prior consent in any form of binding or cover other than that in which it is published and without a similar condition including this condition being imposed on the subsequent publisher.
The moral right of James M. Love has been asserted.
ISBN-13: 9781709757938

In 1982 I was part of 2 Para Group, 4 Field Regt Royal Artillery. I served as the signaller in the Forward Observation Officers Party.

In later years I've spoken to several ex-soldiers who have experienced emotional problems and have been unable to come to terms with what they saw and the events they took part in during their experiences in the South Atlantic during 1982.

My two kids are important to me. I love my daughter Beckie, son Callum, and granddaughter Raynah-Mae to bits. However, I am not very good when it comes to relationships and I have hit a self-destruct button on more than one occasion. I honestly have not really had all that many serious or meaningful relationships in my life. But when I did, I was totally loyal to them and with the ladies concerned totally in love. I served as a soldier for nearly eighteen years with the British Army and worked for them again as a civil servant for another twenty years. In that time, I managed to travel the world and enjoyed myself immensely.

CONTENTS

ACKNOWLEDGMENTS i

POEMS FROM THE ASHES 1

1. My Life, Was Written *3*
2. Sybaritic, But I Promised *4*
3. I Whispered as… *5*
4. All the Colours of a Rainbow? *6*
5. Could You Hear That? *7*
6. I Dream Too *8*
7. I'll Take It *9*
8. Hold Me As I Sleep, and Kiss Me *10*
9. I Kissed, a Myriad, of… Light *11*
10. The Fabric of Our Being, Is *12*
11. Some Promises *13*
12. When *14*
13. 70 Virginis… *15*
14. Did You Ever *16*
15. There Could Never Be *17*
16. 470 Nanometres, It's Just *18*
17. Whisper… *19*
18. I No Longer Cast a Pebble, For *20*
19. The Devilled Bones of *21*
20. Sadness *22*
21. Today It's *23*
22. In Quiet Moments, There's Times *24*
23. Send Me *25*
24. The Setting Sun *26*
25. I Once Tasted… *27*

26. I've Heard It… 28
27. Love Might Touch 29
28. How..30

MOODS OF WAR 31

29. Death's Smokey 33
30. May 82 34
31. Bullets Marked 35
32. A Battle's Roar...36
33. Play it Again Sam, For I'm.....................................37
34. Fitzroy 38
35. In Mud and Filth We Lay and… 39
36. Like a Dante-esque..40
37. A Call To War, a Call To......................................41
38. An Odyssey In 42
39. As Symbolic Whistles Blew 43
40. We Called Out in the Rain....................................44
41. The Gulf, The Ghan, the Middle East.................45
42. May 26th 1982… 46
43. Chronophobia, it's Still and I See Them Row......47
44. 7.62mm… It's Life's Chorus..................................48
45. What Could I Say… To...49
46. Until...50
47. The Wind of War Roared 51
48. What I've Shared, I've Shared..............................52
49. Saddle Up the Horses of the Apocalypse 53
50. You'll Never Know Nor Share 54
51. My Thoughts Stray, To…......................................55
52. Frangere a Malady I 56
53. Sweet Death, We Taste...57

BLOWN BY A CHILL WIND 59

    54. My All... 61
    55. Once Again 62
    56. Me And 63
    57. I'm Mixed Up, Baby.. 64
    58. Just Me, and…... 65
    59. A Whirlwind 66
    60. We're Not Perfect... 67
    61. All That I Know Is… 68
    62. My Soul Felt 69
    63. Such Sweet 70
    64. Clandestine Meetings... 71
    65. Why Am I 72
    66. Wet... 73
    67. Speak Now… For.. 74
    68. What I Want is…... 75
    69. Who… 76
    70. It's Not Cupid's Arrow 77
    71. It Skipped a Beat… 78
    72. Just Another... 79
    73. Ride of The.. 80
    74. When… It's Grey 81
    75. If You Parked Your… Body 82
    76. Questions, Questions… 83
    77. Shhhhhhh 84
    78. Yours Burn, While Mine Are… 85

PTSD MERE WORDS ARE NOT ENOUGH 87

    79. Perhaps Today's, The…... 89
    80. I'm Weary... 90
    81. I'm Off To Bed 92
    82. It's That Kind of Night.. 93

83. Sometimes…	94
84. I Can Laugh, and I Can Cry	95
85. I Often Sit and Stare, But…	96
86. Coming Out	97
87. I dreamt… I'd	98
88. A-mhàin, I'll rest…	99
89. Once again…	100
90. Drinking for…	101
91. Pour Le Dernier Temps	102
92. And I'll Share Your Name	103
93. Just Before You Wake…	104
94. Laisse-Moi Tranquille	105
95. Edvard Munch	106
96. Who Listens…?	107
97. I'm	108
98. I See Them…	109
99. You Know… I Once Knew	110
100. I'm too… old, to sit	111
101. Proverbs, Life, Dreams & Death	112
102. When There's a Skinder on the Wind, of…	113
103. Men Apart…	114
ABOUT THE AUTHOR	115

ACKNOWLEDGMENTS

There are probably lots of people who feel that they are due a mention. Perhaps too many to indeed mention. My words, my emotions, I thank you all for input, helping to further shape the man which is me. Perhaps my next book may contain a definitive list.

POEMS FROM

THE ASHES

1. My Life, Was Written

In a book, that is, on a table,
Found,
In that great hall…
Named,
Valhalla…
Written,
With a thousand-year-old ink.
Which faded, from the page.
Before my name,
Even dried.
We're Family…
I used to think that death,
Mayhap was a punishment.
The thirst of life quenched…
Before I'd drank my fill!
Perhaps I've got it wrong?
Life, may be the punishment!
For with death,
There is no further pain…
After all.

2. Sybaritic, But I Promised

A sensuous pleasure… Perhaps if.
You were to catch me… if,
I'm smiling.
Or even, if… I'm blue!
Perhaps,
You want to share, a… tomorrow.
Or merely…
Just a moment… of my time.
For, right here, for, right now.
And if I got a kiss…
I promise
Not to… tell.

3. I Whispered as...

The darkness called.
And its cries, echoed… in the night.
I'm cold.
No rest, for me.
The rhythmic beating, of… my heart
Is stilled
There's a, chill…
Upon, my soul.
It's a long time, since… I felt,
The wet sand, beneath…
Bare feet.
Or a lover's subtle breath.
Upon
My lips.
There's a sadness in my eyes.
That's killed, the spark.
Life, withers…
For
Death, called out my name.

4. All the Colours of a Rainbow?

The scent of your love.
If I could, just transcend…
Those moments… to a colour
It might be…
The colour, of your eyes.
Of a morning.
Or perhaps…
The colour, of your lips.
Of a moonlit evening.
Or
The colour of… your blushes.
In moments of wanton… passion
Which lingered like a rainbow.
But is all gone now!
Causing my eye to jade.
I no longer know the scent!
Am therefore, am rendered…
Colour blind.
As while I forlornly search,
For that lover's… litany.
And all the while I do…
My current colour, is…
A paler shade of blue.

5. Could You Hear That?

A sound… so fine.
While I slept…
Winds howled,
As waves, smashed!
Upon, many different shores.
And around the world…
Guns roared, and people died.
But above it all…
Was it was only I
Who, heard…
That
A butterfly, was crying?

6. I Dream Too

Life's full of dreams, where…
Childish dreams,
Are meant to fade and die.
Impossible dreams,
Are meant, to fail…
Because we didn't try.
Our worst thought dreams…
Turn into nightmares!
Because love got in the way?
Or we never shared!
Or we cared…
Too
Much.

7. I'll Take It

It's your smile.
I truly, fell in love with!
Its wickedness, reflected…
In your eyes.
A pixie-like voice,
That could command.
Whilst, full of passion
Didst…
Melt, a stony heart.
And caused, a tear… to dwell.
For all my life,
A regret, for all time.
A memory, of love.
To take…
To
My grave.

8. *Hold Me As I Sleep, and Kiss Me*

Just…
Make, sweet love… to me.
Teach me, to… dance!
Meet me… there.
Amongst, the stars!
Take my hand, and… steal my heart.
I, now have the keys… to,
The asylum.
And caused, a tear… to dwell.
So come, and set me free.
Just, share with me, for the moment.
Don't try to understand me.
Don't look too deep.
You won't like… what you see.
Keep the colours loud, and keep them bright.
Drown, reality,
In fizzy wine and froth.
All, I'm asking… of you,
Is…
Tell me, that you love me.
And, be there,
In the morning
When I awake.

9. I Kissed, a Myriad, of… Light

It's just…
How, to kill a wish!
Sometimes a wish, is so obscure.
It lays beyond, the realms, of fantasy.
So we no longer dream, of it… encore.
And once the spirit of loves verse is, lost…
I searched, within a memory.
For a dream.
And saw that girl, from the squat…
That played, the guitar,
So well.
Another… The barmaid…
Not forgetting the redhead, that shaved.
And I only knew…
The true colour of her hair,
Because… she told me.
Long forgotten memories
That happened before, an epic… journey
I once made in life.
And could I ever forget, that…
Summer
In Bexley Heath?

10. *The Fabric of Our Being, Is....*

A letter to Althea?
When I was in jail.
I wrote one similar, from the Traz.
But not four walls…
For one was full of bars.
I washed my clothes, in a sink.
I dried them, hanging
From, my windows…
And they never smelled, more sweeter!
Nor, were any cleaner, than
A free man's
Clothes.

11. Some Promises

Like, drops of rain.
Some run away.
Some form, puddles
Some, wash the tears…
From, your skin.
Others evaporate,
With the warmth, of the sun.
Whilst some fill, and drown…
Your heart.
Or… maybe they just…
Disappear, in the ether.
But, still linger… in the mind.
Some wistful
Some
Too dark, to keep.

12. When

You've seen things,
beyond... the realm,
of reason.
Where, you've lived,
within... a,
twilight world.
Where a dream,
was once... reality.
Though not, necessarily,
a faerie tale.
When life,
no longer,
tastes... sweet.
Nor is, serene.
Fear no evil.
For, I have tread that path.
Spoke with death.
And
We whispered, dead men's words.

13. 70 Virginis...

The ocean rocked... me.
As the waves, pushed me... towards,
The sandy shore.
I'd floated in on, the ebbing tide.
Drifting, on the water.
I'm floating on a sea of pain,
And abject misery.
Just staring, at the sky,
No longer, do I feel, the cold.
Nor hear, the crying of the gulls.
And I'm slowly sinking,
With despair.
In the Goldilocks zone
Eyes... opened... wide.

14. Did You Ever

Kiss, a…
Wisp?
Or taste an exotic drink, they don't make, no more…
Or wish, there was more to life
Than just, foolish whims?
Sombre, are my thoughts.
While my memories, are… murky, black.
You were, that… tree,
Full of, forbidden… fruit!
That was, so lush, once plucked.
I kept going back, for more.
Sweet, was the taste, of sin.
And so I ask…
Why?
And would I
Ever
Know…?

15. There Could Never Be...

Whence on rain-painted streets
Under a waning moon and falling stars
My life and dreams were… shared.
Remembering,
The sparkle in your eyes.
The mischief, in your laugh,
And star shine… from your smile.
All, t'while… I'm missing,
The warmth, of your lips on…
Winter nights.
And how you held me tight.
'Tis no other's heartbeat, I wish to hear.
I long to pass each majik moment, like enchanted lovers, caught in a pleach.
As I could never, share again…
With
…anyone but you!

16. 470 Nanometres, It's Just

If you know her...
Could you, pass this along, from me?
The nights, have grown darker, and... lonelier, now, that you have gone.
I no longer see, a sparkle, in...
Blue eyes.
With which, the twinkling, of the nights stars
I did, once... compare.
The sky, it seems, has now, lost its lustre.
While, I have lost.
My
Lovely eyes...
Of
Blue.

17. Whisper…

My name.
Like, I once, whispered… yours
In the dark, of the night,
While, holding… you close.
Or, when we were apart.
Or when, I felt the want, of your love.
I'll forever whisper your name.
When,
An Angel's feather, touches, my heart.
When I'm melancholy, and feeling lonely.
When I think, I can smell,
your… perfume.
Or I thought I heard your voice, upon the wind.
Your voice is embedded, in my soul.
So just…
Whisper
My name….

18. I No Longer Cast a Pebble, For

I heard the sadness, in your voice.
That showed me, the colour, of…
Your soul.
And it matched, the purity…
Of your eyes.
Oft, I hear, their… silent call.
And wonder…
Should I respond
Or just wait, my turn…?
While in my eyes… there's
A deadness, to match
The colour, of their shrouds.
There's a darkness, that…
Fills my heart.
To catch
Those
Ripples on the pond.

19. The Devilled Bones of

Woe…
The absence, of light.
Once again.
I'm drinking, on my own.
Waiting, for the darkness.
The whisper, of… wings.
Valkyries.
To claim, my soul.
To, take me home.
We're having, a party.
Just me,
'n'
…the dead.

20. Sadness

Rules, my soul.
While my heart, lays waning.
I miss each touch, and every kiss.
And still, my body… lays, wanting.
Love.
Never, more… I'll be.
Not, once more, will I see.
And while my lips, crack, and chafe.
In dreams.
I only think, of those, long… dead.
'N' kiss, lost… forgotten lovers.
Only ever thinking, of the past.
So, my wish, is not, …to dream.
For my past is my future.
And, so it… remains.
Tomorrow, will be, yesterday…
While today, will ever be.
The day preceding… My death.
While
An emotion
Stole my soul…

21. Today It's

Rain…
It rained.
And rained.
And rained.
And it's still
Raining.

22. In Quiet Moments, There's Times

Deep, deep, down…

Beyond, where I think, and I can see.
Where lies a memory,
That haunts, my tears.
And, every now, and when.
For some unknown… reason.
One, escapes my eye, and flows.
And sadness fills me.
For, I know… not.
Why
I cry…

23. Send Me

Flowers,
For… I love.
Their vibrant colours, and
Their, sweet, scent.
For, I miss my love,
And, the colours…
She didst bring!
And just like her, they'll not long, last.
But, a brief beauty…
Full of life, before they wilt,
And die
But, while they're here
They'll be …mine!
My tears are real.
But my dreams, are made… of, smoke!
Which have dissipated, in the wind.
Like a fallen rainbow.
Like the discarded petals.
Of, my now…
Dead
Flowers.

24. The Setting Sun

Melds the horizon.
As, moistened eyes, now mist my vision.
I've forgotten, most… of what I've seen.'
While daylight hints, of fresh delights.
'Tis the darkness of the night
Whose sombre song…
Reeks, death's melodious, tones.
To steal away…
Souls…
Before the dawn!

25. I Once Tasted…

Freedom, long ago.
And…
It was sweet, and like, no… other.
'Cept, perhaps, that… of love.
Though…
Now not for me… I'll no longer seek that spice
Of life.
It brings no joy.
For it left bitter, splenetic reminder.
A taint, that spoiled fruit, doth sometimes have.
That permeates a soul.
And…

26. I've Heard It…

When a dead man, sings.
And it's sweeter, than…
Life itself.
Where time
Has no limits, nor… conceptions.
When music, fills, my… being.
Let the music, move you,
Like it, sways… my soul!
There is no glory, in dying.
There never has, and never will!
So live today,
Like, there's …no tomorrow.
Live it wild, and
Live it
Loud…!

27. Love Might Touch

But not.
When you're dead.
For when you're dead.
You've left, pain behind.
The colours, all, gone.
'Cept… Black.
The black, will always, remain.
I've been left, all… alone.
Searching, for that someone.
Who's, somewhere.
Who's been absorbed, by the night.
Beyond the vision of my sight.
And thus, is rendered invisible.
To
My heart…

28. How

What manner...
Could, a melancholy song,
Still my heart.
But not, stop... my tears?
Could, a tender moment, last, forever?
If so... how would.
A brotherly act
Laying heavy, on the soul...
Outlive, a love... or, true romance?
Too many questions, that, no one... hears.
My words, only echoing...
While
I'm talking, to the bottom... of,
A glass.
So
Say you...?

MOODS OF WAR

29. Death's Smokey

Cloud…
Smoke filled my eyes,
Burned my lungs…
Took away the colours,
Turned it all to grey.
It moved within the wind.
Leaving behind,
Blackened remains.
It clung to my clothes
Like a cape, made in hell.
It's an image, I try to forget.
But it's hard.
For, whenever I see, grey smoke.
I remember…
That
Smell…

30. May 82

It rained,
And I heard it fall.
Maybe not every drop…
But almost all.
We cut the turf,
And stacked it high.
Two foot thick,
And just as wide.
Rain ran down my face,
While it filled the hole.
Soaked my clothes,
Washed my soul.
No gentle pitter-patter this,
It crashed.
The wind howled and blew,
As the bayonets slashed.
All the while,
Eight thousand miles away.
You cheered…
Got drunk,
And slept
In a cosy warm bed.

31. Bullets Marked

Some buzzed…
While others, whizzed.
I felt their breath…
And I, shrank smaller.
Though, lots passed…
And I never,
…heard a sound.
But I saw, where they went.
I saw…
Who… they found.

32. A Battle's Roar

Simply, music…
To my ears.
So, sing your songs, and…
Beat your drums.
To the staccato, rock 'n' roll…
My lungs are full cordite,
While my head's filled, with,
The whispering sound.
Of the, gimpy's… roar!
It's in sync, with the crump, 'n' thump,
Of the falling, of… the shot.
Of dirt, and dust, and sandy graves.
Rewards… just bits of tin…
A symphony of sound.
A lousy lullaby…
To help you sleep.
When…
Faraway
In foreign lands…

33. Play it Again Sam, For I'm

Stirring stuff, they played…
As we march along.
We are singing… dead men's songs…
Melodies… centuries old.
Of flesh and bones,
That create bonds.
Where we empathise with,
Deeds of glory…
Of which are merely,
Heroic tales that only tell half our story.
Lullabies or crooning
Crude, raucous or dreaming.
We are writing history…
My friends.
Blood-soaked minutes, every one.
The booze burns…
As it goes down.
And fists smash the table.
We sing, and drink, and chant!
For those dead, gone, and
Unable.

34. Fitzroy

Low and fast,
That's how they came.
Screaming low across the ground…
I swear.
If I'd tried.
I could have touched it, as it passed.
A trail of death and devastation,
They'd left behind.
Where the rising black plumes of smoke,
Lay testament to that.
The dead, the maimed,
Trapped on a floating inferno.
In that brief moment.
Fathers, sons and brothers, died.
The lucky ones that lived.
Bleeding, burnt and scarred, shocked.
Not now, the men I once knew.

Author's Notes/Comments:
I can always visualise the grinning Sky Hawk pilot as he passed.

35. In Mud and Filth We Lay and...

To be proud of someone.
You need to know, what they've done!
As the horsemen of the apocalypse waited...
A warrior's heart, from another time... Lay dormant.
Trying, to make sense, of earthly, realities.
Like a dog...
That's caught, a scent... on the wind.
It sparked.
While they spoke in Sogdian.
They smiled, that macabre grin.
With a Fibonacci rose, upon...
Their chests.
Skeletal mounts, pawed the ground,
Biding... their time.
Their riders grotesque laugh cut across the wind.
And sent a shiver, down the spine.
Of every man.
And still...
We
Waited... for the dawn.

36. Like a Dante-esque

Death's Call.
It screamed... like,
A banshee's... wail...
Its breath...
It pushed... my chest, so hard.
It touched, my spine.
Time, stopped still... for a, moment.
While an eerie silence reigned.
Then, the ground erupted!
Fire and molten metal shards
Cut through the air.
Bringing further screams, from the maimed, and dying.
Adding, voices to...
Hell's
Choir.

37. A Call To War, a Call To

There's a greyish-ness to the dawn.
When black, slips… to blue.
Where the obscure, lays, in between…
Where death, hones… his scythe.
Where there is, a… stillness.
Where oft, soldiers pause,
And reflect.
There are no words…
Before the coming of the dawn.
Nor sounds, 'cept, of the dead man's, whistle!
The prelude…
To
Death.

38. An Odyssey In

I had no taste,
For my mouth was dry.
My empty stomach…
Knotted from its pit.
I felt no fear…
Nor never felt, the cold!
The night was still…
But not for long.
Soon to be heard,
Was the pale horses' song.
And death swept down amidst,
The screaming shells…
Whilst Valkyries,
Took their choice.
Brave men lived, and died,
While we let our bullets fly.
On those mountains,
During June.
In
1982.

39. As Symbolic Whistles Blew

Side by side, we lay.
Within an arm's distance.
Prelude, to a dawn…
Each man's thoughts… his own.
No sound, save the wind.
Which brought that battle's din.
All lost within… blue grey black,
Death's favourite colour.
A mountain to climb
Just beyond the river.
Soon we'll see the sun.
Soon well get up run…
Soon it will be over.
Soon we'd…
Dance to
Death's soulful tune.

40. We Called Out in the Rain

It cut, like a thousand knives.
It bit deep.
While invisible fingers tore and…
And tried to rip us, off our feet.
Skin… turned blue, then grey.
Like how the skies, colour changed.
And love left our hearts…
True emotion replaced by
Duty… and devotion.
Only,
To one another.

41. The Gulf, The Ghan, the Middle East

I looked at the devastation.
The pictures of the maimed.
Headlines that screamed…!
For the dead it portrayed.
"But it's not my war!" I said.
Mine had fields of yellow, blue vistas.
We fought for Britain, and its crown.
But you'd not know that…
But I still hear the gunfire, the shellfire,
And the bombs.
Though I no longer stand amidst…
Those windswept, fields of gold.
A part of my heart, is always… there!
For that was my war…
And it was a bit further south.

42. May 26th 1982…

It shut out the sun, turning the sky black.
It gathered impetuous pushing them over,
malevolently…
Like a roaring express train, loosened from its
tracks…
Careering wildly, across fields.
Its force… striking at exposed flesh
Pummelling bodies, knocking them over like skittles.
Winter, had arrived…
On the fifth day it snowed.

43. Chronophobia, it's Still and

I See Them Row

I can't wait,
For the coming snows…
To cleanse my soul…
I trade, in times, of secrets…
Of the deeds, of the dead.
With only those, who knows?
When grey skies, turn black.
And winter's chills, call…
It's the devil, who's…
Trying to claim, your soul.
While the skies change, again.
Black to grey, and then, to bluish white.
Snowflakes swirl…
Like the screams, of the dying.
They envelope your body, and stick.
Drowning out reality.
Soaking lashes, blinding all who see.
Draining life.
I'll always remember.
Each time, it snows.
Snow… cladding, corpses…
Lying there
Row
On row.

44. 7.62mm… It's Life's Chorus

I like, the oily cold feel of the metal.
The menacing, blue black sheen.
As it slowly warms… in…
My hands.
It's a comforting weight…
It moulds… to my soul.
Like Judas, it holds twenty!
It's an international currency,
Pointed, copper coated…
…bits of lead.
That crack and thump,
800 feet per second…
…as they, pass through the air.
That whizz 'n' splat… it takes…
Its pound of flesh.
As it tears its way, on its path.
Fist-size holes appear.
Delivering, its…
Message
Of Death.

45. What Could I Say... To

For...
I have seen the likes,
That, few, have ever seen...
I've inhaled,
the breath,
from
A dying man's... last words.
I've been immersed, in the van of battle.
I've watched dispassionately.
While brothers died.
I shared Death's banquet.
I've seen the sun... bloody red, whilst it set.
Never, expecting to see it, rise.
I have learned the truth, about... dying,
And the cost,
To men, at war.
I've tasted cordite, mingled with fear.
Death has no pact with destiny.
And I'm drinking with,
the lost,
the forgotten,
and the dead.
I've saved the world
And it's been inherited
By
The snowflakes, from hell.

46. Until

Until you have had the ground,
beneath your feet,
disappear.
Seen the sky, turn black,
and, shower you… with,
molten metal fragments.
You'll never know, how precious,
the morning can be,
for men, at war
I pray you never have to
share the moment.

47. The Wind of War Roared

Not me…
And
I screamed…
And I ran, faster.
Not me
And, I laughed…
While, on I zigged.
Then, I zagged.
The tears, streaked…
My cheeks.
And the air, was… filled.
With lead
My lungs burned.
As the smoke.
Blocked out the sun.
I was down.
Then…
I pushed myself up again.
And
I began to run…

48. What I've Shared, I've Shared

Earth, sand, and mud.
From holes, all over the world.
We'd stare, at the skies, and stars…
Share our secrets, trade our desires.
Thinking of home, wherever that was.
Thinking of those we loved…
Of those, we'd hope to meet.
Hoping not to die.
There was a calmness, amidst it all.
A silent longing…
An empathy, greater than any other.
For,
I shared those holes
With my airborne brothers.

49. Saddle Up the Horses of the Apocalypse

My arcs aren't clear… yet.
All this I see before me…
It's… my life…!
I've done a three-metre check,
Death's got my six.
"P hour", may still remain… undecided.
But I've already crossed life's start line!
We'll be going in hot.
Though the enemy strength unclear.
It won't be clean fatigue.
From the DZ to the feba.
I'll continue to tab, till I hit that FRV.
What I do know…
I won't be alone!
Standby, brothers… and get ready,
To open the gates of "Valhalla".
We're going home!

50. You'll Never Know Nor Share

I'm just sad.
Because I can't,
Share…
No words…
No thoughts…
You weren't there!
How can you say?
You know…
Did you,
See his head explode?
Or feel the spray of blood
As it hit your face?
Never to forget
No semblance of a
Cloth
Only in darker times
Can you…
Feel it all.
Like yesterday!

Extract from the diaries of "Jock Love A Soldier & A Poet : In The Field of Battle: Times Were Harsh".

51. My Thoughts Stray, To...

Darkness.
Don't pray for me…
I'm past redemption…
My deeds, outweigh my faith.
I'll languish… in that great hall.
Drinking,
With my brothers.
Until that final battle.
Dead men, can't die.
My love now lies, immortal.
And lonely now I sit.
Waiting for that war.
They call
Ragnarök…

52. Frangere a Malady I

Need to know.
Doctor, doctor…
Can you tell me why…?
I'm drinking vodka,
Trying to drown away, my sleep!
And why
There are no songs, that laud my friends.
Through the memories, still run deep.
And though you think, I'm listening to you…
Even while you speak.
I'm 8 thousand miles away…
On a southern, summer's day.
At bottom, of, the world…
I'm toasting warriors.
And the moment, makes me smile.
I see them all, just like, yesterday.
Then I see them as they fall.
When I'm alone at night.
Their silent screams invade my dreams.
Preventing me from sleep.
I saw death in all his forms.
And though he passed me by.
I have a bond, with brothers,
That even death
Can't break.

53. Sweet Death, We Taste...

Come sweet death,
Bringer of the dawn.
Leave me tranquil…
While innocents, sleep.
Come sweet death,
Harvester, of light.
Show me the path,
Through, the darkest of night.
Come sweet death…
Your warm, embrace.
Turns to ice, at spider's touch.
While the dying, says it all.
Come sweet death…
Our mission of life,
Tainted, by the smell,
Of…
Our own blood.

BLOWN BY A CHILL WIND

54. My All....

And if I had one wish…
I'd wish for you!
And if it were a dream…
I'd only dream… of you!
And if…
I'd had to forfeit,
My meagre life?
I'd gladly give it
For you…

55. Once Again

I've seen…
A rainbow!
And now…
I believe…
In fairy tales!
I believe
In majik!
For,
I've found myself…
A princess!
And I'm
So totally…
In Love.

56. Me And

You have that something…
That, I don't know what?
That…
Je ne c'est quoi?
That unknown quality,
That lies underneath.
Below the surface,
Unseen…
Like the North Pole,
Magnetism!
An animal attraction?
In a simple, pure,
Demure… kind of way.
All I know is…
I've been,
Drawn… to
You!

57. I'm Mixed Up, Baby....

I misinterpret, daily,
My lover's ...thoughts.
And perhaps ...sometimes,
Her dreams. I never seem,
To comprehend.
Of what, she really
Wants or needs.
My heart is hers...
And should she
Choose to listen.
It beats with a will,
And a passion,
That's for her
All, Alone.

58. Just Me, and…

I'm thinking of,
A pair…
Of silky thighs…
Sweet cherry lips.
Sensual, blue eyes.
Of a moment…
Ne'er replaced!
I'm thinking.
Of,
You…

59. A Whirlwind

Bright eyes, mirroring blue eyes.
Where dreams have met the shore.
Life's expectations, turned to sand…
Toto, it ain't Kansas, anymore…!
Romance.

60. We're Not Perfect

I think that's why…
We're all chasing rainbows.
Why we all search the sky…
At times… we
Try to catch moon beams,
While we reach for the stars.
A tentative stab at reality.
While our dreams…
Melt around us.
Expectations swirling,
Down a sink.
Sometimes…
Angels do… crash and burn too.

61. All That I Know Is...

I see you in the morn.
As you stretch,
Stifle a yawn...
Curl up again,
And lick your lips.
I've seen the mischief...
In your eyes.
Felt your body's warmth.
Touched the heat,
From your thighs.
Tasted that probing tongue.
All the while,
Just
Knowing...
You were mine.

62. My Soul Felt

I cast a tear
Into, that internal void
That some call love…
In hope
It heals
A broken heart
Which calls to me
A Chill.

63. Such Sweet

What heart
Of any man
Could but deny…
A blown kiss
From a cherub's
Lips?

64. Clandestine Meetings...

A telephone… is a mere,
Conduit.
To another place…
Which steals…
A moment of you time.
Via voice, and buried wires,
Where dark secrets may linger…
Or sweet secrets, of promise,
Can be murmured.
So a date, a rendezvous,
In the dark of the night…
May take place.

65. Why Am I

I'm listening to the radio
And I've heard a song
That's made me cry…
It made me think of you
And of all that I was missing.
Nature's ganging up on me,
The sky's the colour of your eyes
The leaves the colour of your hair
I swear to God
I smell your fragrance in the air
All I'm left with
Are memories.
Life
Is so fucking unfair
It's you I want to be with.
Alone again?

66. Wet

Wakey… wakey,
Sweet kitten.
I'm home, once more…
While lost dreams lay…
Crushed, upon the floor.
For Daddy drank with Vikings,
Last night!
He ate all the leaves, from…
Læraðr.
And now, he'd like…
To claim
His prize… I hope
Perhaps it's still moist.

67. Speak Now... For

I shed a tear... for,
foolishness.
And the silence...
that I kept.
Which caused...
my true love,
To be...
forever lost.
And so,
I now languish alone.

68. What I Want is…

I'd love… to,
feel your shoulder,
lean on mine…
Intertwine our fingers,
Hold your hand…
Feel your body move,
as you breathe.
Watch your breasts…
sink and rise.
See that little vein,
in your neck… pulse.
Feel your body's warmth.
Touch your soul.
Steal your heart.
Oh Vienna!
I'd love to…
Chill.

69. Who…

When I'm long gone.
With my ashes,
In the breeze…
If an oft not spoken word,
Or a forgotten turn of phrase.
Should make you pause…
For thought.
Please take a moment,
And think of…
Me?

70. It's Not Cupid's Arrow

You went and… stole my heart!
Then you ripped it,
Right in two…
We'd spent the night together.
But now that the morning's here
What else…
Are you gonna do?
If I even tried to run,
Would I make it out that door?
I'm so darned confused
I don't know…
what, to do
anymore!

71. It Skipped a Beat...

There was a light knock,
At the door.
As I opened it…
Framed, in the doorway.
Stood a siren!
Pure sol
And my heart… hammered
Within my chest.

72. Just Another

I cried a thousand tears,
To drown, in a pool of apathy.
Whence, chance meeting…
Of fair lady… now,
Ended… with sweet sorrow.
At the parting of our ways,
My love has gone…
And I am a crushed,
As a flower underfoot!
Trodden upon unmercifully,
In the cold light
Of
Day?

73. Ride of The

Warriors are we!
Guardians of destiny.
Love lost men…
from all,
The kingdoms.
Battle hardened on that field…
Though lost,
In lace and perfume!
Fit only for…
Death… and the,
Valkyries!

74. When... It's Grey

I want to walk that beach.
And I'd love to hold, your hand.
Silver puddles... of salty water...
Glittering... upon the sand.
To feel, my heart lift...
Like a gull, upon the wind.
See your smile,
Dancing... in... your eyes.
To steal a kiss...
'Neath,
A chill...
December sky.

75. If You Parked Your... Body

Could I kiss, your sweet lips?
Could I hold, your body...
Close to mine?
Would it be a chance meet?
A moment in passing...
Or a planned moment in time?
Would lust, win over love,
Or would there be a blossom...
That I could cherish?
Savour, and refine.
Would you put,
Your sweet lips...
Next to mine?

76. Questions, Questions...

What lays hidden,
'neath those clothes?
What guise…
does your body take?
Does it have adornments?
Tattoos perhaps,
Or are you pierced?
What lays hidden…
'neath those folds?
What majik…
have you inked,
upon your naked… torso?
What's been pinned?
Questions.

77. Shhhhhhh

Say not a word…
I want to hold you tight
No… I lie…
I want to crush your body
Close to mine
I want to flood you
Full of… emotion
I want the heat from your… thighs
To warm my heart
I want to kindle a spark.

78. Yours Burn, While Mine Are...

In the vastness… of the darkness.
I reached out, for you…
But once again…
Like my dreams,
You were gone!
But I cried…
Only,
Silent tears.

PTSD MERE WORDS ARE NOT ENOUGH

79. Perhaps Today's, The...

It's just for me, and,
I hear a call…
From, those long lost…
And those, just gone.
With whom, I share a bond.
Lost souls…
Brave men, brothers true.
Which creates a longing
Which fills my heart.
Which is a love spurned void.
And their calling,
Gets, that little bit louder.
Every single…
Day!

80. I'm Weary

A long, long time, weary… and,
lonely.
I'm just waiting for the dawn…
I'm drunk, yet again,
and all alone.
Lost, within the darkness.
Where, there's no one to hold me.
Where then, was all that joy,
that daylight… brought?
It's all gone now.
I've seen some bad times.
I've seen, some good ones.
I don't know which,
outweighs,
which.
But both memories.
Can make me cry.
Or laugh, like… a loon.
Forget all.
All… that, I had.
I wish, for what… I can't have.
And no one, will… ever know.
Or share.
Of the vistas, that I've seen.
Nor the silence, I once heard.
That was only broken,
by their screams.

By death, and the dying,
The maimed, and the long-time dead.
Being immortalised only,
From the images, in my head.

81. I'm Off To Bed

To search, for forgotten dreams.
For aspirations, that were never... realised.
For they all died, within the night...
I know not now...
what I chase,
when
darkness calls.

82. It's That Kind of Night

Where… there's.
No one, to talk to.
No one, to call…
No one, to hug.
Not even, a hand, to…hold.
No lips with which to seek,
Succour.
I'm beyond forlorn.
For no apparent, reason.
I'm feeling…
Lugubrious,
in a fairly melancholy,
bottomless,
kind of empty heart.
Sort, of way.
And I'm feeling sad.

83. Sometimes…

I cry for your happiness.
Sometimes…
I cry, when I'm sad…
Once upon a time.
I had no tears, for anyone.
Not even, myself.
It seems that dreams,
Are non-legally binding.
Sometimes
It's lamentable.

84. I Can Laugh, and I Can Cry

All…
At the same time.
Mostly, when trying to drown myself…
From the inside… out.
And vodka, is the choice of my tears.
The smiles that I have,
The ones I can't share!
For they're drunken, and… stupid.
And all mine
And nobody cares!!

85. I Often Sit and Stare, But...

I couldn't focus on a single time.
Nor separate from my emotions.
Of whence, a thought occurred…
That didn't bring a tear,
Nor resurrect an image…
That was burned upon my brain.
Though…
You will never see it!

86. Coming Out

Trouble, me…
no,
more…
Black… dreams,
of death.
I'm nearly done.
You'll have me, soon enough.
But on my terms.
I'll choose my place.
I'll choose my day.
You may win…
In the end.
But my life's
My game
To play…

87. I dreamt… I'd

I could sleep.
But, I was wrong.
The scent of fresh linen…
Pervades, all my dreams.
And brought, the sensation…
Of
Desire.
Of being clean, of a wish to taste.
To dine, of love's pleasures.
I can always scream…
Or so
I've been told.
A memory, I'd once forgot.
Surfacing for, no apparent reason.
Not for life, or love's pleasures.
It's a lonely bed…
For a man…
Who's been, to war.
And whose
Dreams have
Died…

88. *A-mhàin, I'll rest...*

I don't sleep, so good, these days.
Furry tongued, dry of mouth.
I taste the dawn…
Of each, and every, day.
Though my sheets are cool,
And tender, was… your touch.
'Tis alcohol and its vapours
That calms my mind.
I fight my demons in the dark…
As I slowly sink, into the abyss, called sleep.
There's no need to remind me
Of war and all its horrors.
For I visit its hellish realms each night.
Where I fight and claw my way back,
Towards the light of day.
And all the while, I wake…
alone.

89. Once again…

My feet, remind me
Of when, I was once so cold.
Of a time, I once went to war…
Of those who fell.
And, stayed down.
Never again, to rise…
Of their own accord.
Lonely… is their slumber.
Forgotten, are their deeds.
Their dreams, now… eternal.
Their bones, turned… to dust.
While my soul is ever,
Joined… with theirs.
My body, languishes.
It's an ache,
Of which…
I don't speak.
For, it is of the heart.
And although it has no cure.
It burns the soul,
And
It burns it deep.
It's a malady, which can kill.
But only if…
You don't
Fight back.

90. Drinking for...

Tomorrows
Now my yesterdays, are gone.
When dreams have turned…
To dust.
One last, promise.
Then I'm done.
I have been left, upon… the cusp.
If life could shelter me, from…
Emotions.
How sweet then my dreams, would be.
And promise, would hold,
No…
Reward.

91. Pour Le Dernier Temps

One day I'll close my eyes,
Pour Le Dernier Temps!
Who knows…
What that memorable image may be.
Le miroir de notre âme.
For the last time…

92. And I'll Share Your Name

With
Loneliness.
And the darkness…
That, it brings.
Cold creeps in.
And the silence roars.
Opaque milky eyes
Replace, the lustre.
I once felt.
And I see no future…
Written
In the stars.

93. Just Before You Wake...

You hang between a void.
Where darkness fills your mind,
Your heart, and all your being...
The greyness of the false dawn,
Like a prelude of your life.
Where you are neither,
One thing... or the other.
As you strain to grasp reality.
From a world, you are not yet part of.
You are all alone.
So you hold true, to your wish...
That you could sleep forever!

94. Laisse-Moi Tranquille

Some say, I have a way.
And am good with words!
But if I could rid me now…
Of these scribblings
Of this constant verse.
Of which I find, hurts my head,
Invades my mind.
It's not a gift…
But a mill stone
…round my neck.
Methinks a parody, of a sad
And lonely man
Who's a victim of a curse.
To be left alone.

95. Edvard Munch

Once done a painting.
That, depicted... it well.
The "Silent Scream".
That came... from hell!
All seeing, non-hearing,
He knew my world.
He... knew it... well.
My scrawl of words,
From within... a dream.
Like Edvard Munch,
And
His scream.

96. Who Listens…?

Please Lord,
Could I just die?
I'm not asking for riches…
Nor understanding, or forgiveness.
I've just had enough…
Of all this inane pain,
Of being on the planet…
Of playing this game.
So what do you say Lord,
Do we have deal?
Can I just close my eyes,
Slip away…
And die?

97. I'm

In, that drunken, happy... place!
Before that place, called sleep.
Where I'd like to remain...
To just, drift...
Be, unaccountable.
To taste, a dream... Every time,
I lick my lips.
Wake me, when, the planet's... cries.
Have touched, your soul.
When the seas, are full.
When the ice, is all gone.
And when, the crushing pain,
Within... my head.
Has been, washed
Away...

98. I See Them…

As,
They… see me.
And although they beckon…
They don't yet, speak.
Their silent, screams.
Only echo, in my head.
And in, my nightmares.
The dead…
Are
Forming queues…

99. You Know... I Once Knew

Once upon a time.
And
I really did, give a shit...
And now, there's... only,
The music, in my head.
That echoes of the night.
When all else, is hushed, asleep.
The great undisturbed.
That, non-disputed time.
When death roams unchallenged.
Where, no one cares!
Because, they... can't hear.
The screams, he brings.
They're oblivious to fear.
Lost... within
Their dreams.

100. I'm too... old, to sit

To listen to lullabies.
To comfort me and aid my sleep.
Or have the touch of soft hands…
Soothe my brow.
'Tis alcohol I need!
To slay my demons, and kill my dreams.
For, there's a wish out there…
Somewhere, in the void.
That's been forgotten…
And it lays within the dust.
In the midst, of dead men's bones.
And drink-fuelled conversations.
Where melancholy, is my want.
Where the shadows of heroes
Are long and dark
And I am lost
Amongst the darkness.

101. Proverbs, Life, Dreams & Death

Its oft been said…
you can die in a dream!
And having once…
had those kind of dreams.
I believed it all true.
So,
that's when it all started again
Why,
I let the violent ones resurface.
To just give in,
slip away in your sleep.
No effort…
no mess…
Simply close your eyes
…and dream.

102. When There's a Skinder on the Wind, of...

Distant, forgotten memories.
When sadness, rips your heart apart.
And distant laughter, echoes…
Lonely… is the night!
While silence, haunts the darkness.
How I long, for your touch.
Kiss me and end my tears
Hold me close, and whisper, that…
You love me.
I'm full of angst, and the night, looms encore.
I was rich with knowledge,
For… I've talked with death
I'd been, to
War.

103. Men Apart…

I need to learn, guitar.
So I can play, my brother's song.
To share, the long-dead words…
And the love, once had.
Such a beautiful,
soulful song… a
Melodic… tune.
That resonates, within…
my heart, and plays…
Encore.
Within, my head.
I'm humbled, and… sad.
Of, the experiences of life.
For the people I've met.
For the places I've been,
And… the things, that I've done.
That, they've… never seen.
How fragile, is my heart.
How, strong is our bond.
Of those from long ago.
Of the dead and the maimed.
Of men from a war, now,
never… the same.
Of men apart.
Of Forgotten heroes.
Nay never Forgotten
And Emperors all.

ABOUT THE AUTHOR

Jim was born in Glasgow on 31 March 1955. After a brief spell in the City of Glasgow Police, he joined the Army in 1973 and, in 1974, volunteered for Parachute training. Upon passing P Company and on completion of his jump training, Jim joined 'I' Parachute Battery, Bull's Troop, 7th Parachute Regiment, Royal Horse Artillery.

In 1979, Jim disappeared whilst in BAOR, Germany, and joined the French Foreign Legion where he made the rank of Corporal. Unfortunately, the pay and conditions were not the greatest and Jim decided to "leave" and re-join the British Army. After getting out of France, he hitchhiked back to Osnabruck in West Germany where his unit was then stationed – walking the last 80 kilometres in a blizzard.

After being tried by Court-Martial (under Section 38 of the Army Act 1955), Jim served 7 months and 11 days of his subsequent sentence (6 weeks of it in solitary) having earned 3 months and 4 days remission of sentence for good behaviour. He returned to Aldershot and joined the Parachute contingent of 4th Field Regiment Royal Artillery and was attached initially to B Company of the 2nd Battalion The Parachute Regiment as a member of the Forward Observation Party (as a signaller directing artillery fire).

Jim was then transferred to A Company whilst on top of Sussex Mountains in the Falkland Islands in May 1982 and served on attachment to that unit until

June 1982 when the unit returned to the Battery (29 Corunna 4th Field Regiment, Royal Artillery) and 2 Para sailed home to the UK on the "Norland". Jim's detachment flew out some weeks later. They had been assigned to guard the Argentine General Menendez and the other Argentinean prisoners on the "St Edmund" ferry.

Having bought himself out of the Army in 1991 for £200, Jim is now employed by the Ministry of Defence Guard Service as part of the internal security team at Tedworth House in Wiltshire – a facility run by Help for Heroes in conjunction with the MOD, for Wounded Injured Soldiers and Veterans.

Printed in Great Britain
by Amazon